7·유7($\frac{4}{16}$)

6/18 7·ㄴ4/16

7율 (α : 4/2016)

MAPS and CITIES

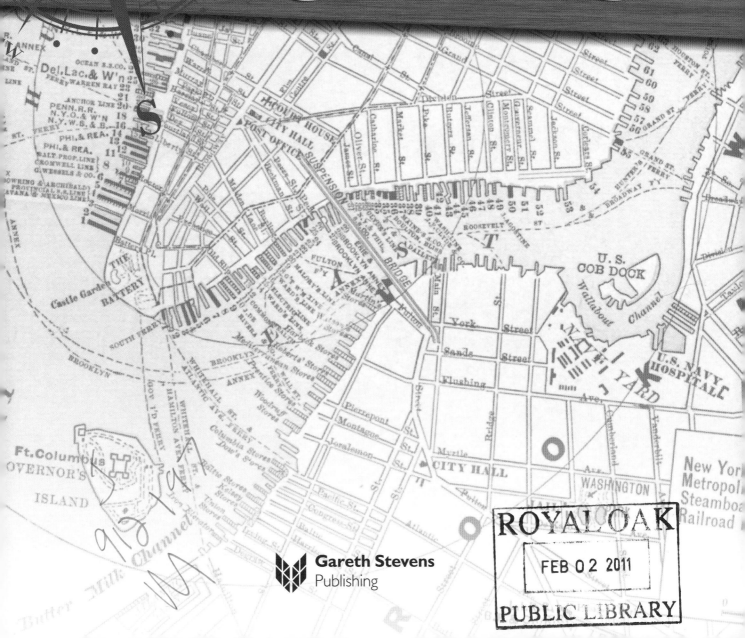

Gareth Stevens
Publishing

Please visit our Web site www.garethstevens.com. For a free color catalog of all our high-quality books, call toll free 1-800-542-2595 or fax 1-877-542-2596.

Library of Congress Cataloging-in-Publication Data
Maps and cities / Tim Cooke, editor.
        p. cm. -- (Understanding maps of our world)
    Includes index.
    ISBN 978-1-4339-3518-3 (library binding) -- ISBN 978-1-4339-3519-0 (pbk.)
    ISBN 978-1-4339-3520-6 (6-pack)
    1. Cities and towns--Maps. 2. Urban geography. I. Cooke, Tim.
    G1028.M37 2010
    912'.19732--dc22

                                                                    2009039223

Published in 2010 by
Gareth Stevens Publishing
111 East 14th Street, Suite 349
New York, NY 10003

© 2010 The Brown Reference Group Ltd.

For Gareth Stevens Publishing:
Art Direction: Haley Harasymiw
Editorial Direction: Kerri O'Donnell

For The Brown Reference Group Ltd:
Editorial Director: Lindsey Lowe
Managing Editor: Tim Cooke
Children's Publisher: Anne O'Daly
Design Manager: David Poole
Designer: Simon Morse
Production Director: Alastair Gourlay
Picture Manager: Sophie Mortimer
Picture Researcher: Clare Newman

3 9082 11748 3969

Picture Credits:
Front Cover: Shutterstock: Oleg Babich b; Kenneth V. Pilon

Brown Reference Group: all artwork

The British Library: 13; Corbis: Bettmann 16/17; Alinari Fratelli 14; DigitalVision: 4m, 4b; Getty Images: Comstock 18; iStock: Robert Bremec 16b; Jupiter Images: Ablestock 5m,15; Photos.com 8, 22; Stockxpert 5t, 34, 39; London Transport: 36; NASA: Landsat 40; Shutterstock: Vladislav Gurfinkel 4t; Amy Nichole Harris 42; Jan Kranendonk 38; Masik 7; Nialat 43; Joel Shawn 9; Steven Wright 5b; Gary Yim 31b, 44

Publisher's note to educators and parents: Our editors have carefully reviewed the Web sites that appear on p. 46 to ensure that they are suitable for students. Many Web sites change frequently, however, and we cannot guarantee that a site's future contents will continue to meet our high standards of quality and educational value. Be advised that students should be closely supervised whenever they access the Internet.

Manufactured in the United States of America
1 2 3 4 5 6 7 8 9   12 11 10

CPSIA compliance information: Batch #BRW0102GS: For further information contact Gareth Stevens, New York, New York at 1-800-542-2595.

Contents

The Changing Shape of the World

1400

This map shows the world known to Europeans in the fifteenth century: Europe and parts of Asia and Africa.

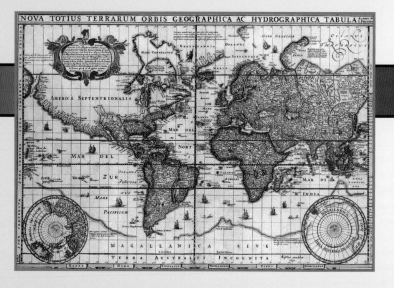

1700

1600

In this seventeenth-century map, only the interior of North America and the southern oceans remain empty.

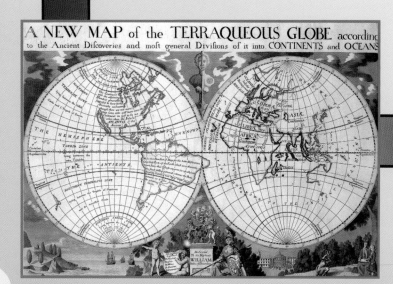

1800

This map reveals more information about Australia, but the northwest coast of North America and most of the Pacific Ocean remain unknown.

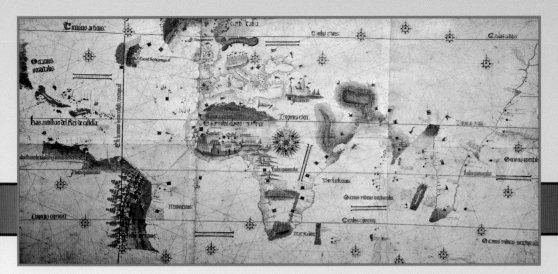

This sixteenth-century map fills in the coasts of Africa and India, the Caribbean islands, and parts of South America.

In this sixteenth-century map, South America is only roughly shaped; the northwest coast of Australia has become part of the legendary "southern continent."

The first photographs of Earth from space were taken only in the 1960s.

1900

This world map was drawn in 1875, when Europeans were at the height of claiming colonies in other lands.

5

Introduction

This is a volume from the set Understanding Maps of Our World. This book looks at how maps and mapping help travelers find their way.

UNDERSTANDING MAPS OF OUR WORLD IS AN eight-volume set that describes the history of cartography, discusses its importance in different cultures, and explains how it is done. Cartography is the technique of compiling information for, and then drawing, maps or charts. Each volume in the set examines a particular aspect of mapping and uses numerous artworks and photographs to help the reader understand the sometimes complex themes.

After all, cartography is both a science and an art. It has existed since before words were written down and today uses the most up-to-date computer technology and imaging systems. Advances in mapmaking through history have been closely involved with wider advances in science and technology. Studying maps demands some understanding of math and at the same time an appreciation of visual creativity. Such a subject is bound to get a little complex at times!

About This Book

This book looks at the different approaches that cartographers have used to tackle the difficult task of mapping cities. The urban landscape is very complex, and modern cities expand upward as well as outward, something the cartographer sometimes has to try and record. People have been living in cities for thousands of years, so this volume looks at historical city maps from the Roman, Chinese, and Japanese empires to show how towns were mapped in the past. The maps produced today are not only used by tourists. Scientists studying disease and poverty and planners in charge of developing the shape of cities also require city maps.

The island of Manhattan, in New York City. The densely packed tall buildings of modern Western cities present a number of difficulties to mapmakers. How do you represent all these tall buildings on a map?

The First Cities

The words for "city" and "civilization" both come from the Latin word civitas *meaning citizenship or state. Maps have helped cities grow and are used to plan them now.*

CITIES WERE MADE POSSIBLE BY AGRICULTURE. Farming enabled the creation of permanent settlements that could produce more food than they needed to survive. This surplus food allowed some people to become specialists in certain skills. Instead of farming or hunting, these skilled individuals traded services or goods for the food that others produced.

During the fourth century B.C. in Mesopotamia (modern-day Iraq), farmers built a small settlement by the Euphrates River. By 2900 B.C., the village had developed into a city called Ur. It was one of the very first groupings of people and buildings that we would recognize as a city, though it was smaller than any of today's cities.

The city became a center for trade. The area around Ur had few natural resources. So the people of the city traded for metals and

NORTHERN PART OF CITADEL

bath

granary

stair

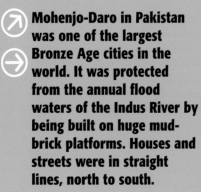

⊘ ➔ **Mohenjo-Daro in Pakistan was one of the largest Bronze Age cities in the world. It was protected from the annual flood waters of the Indus River by being built on huge mud-brick platforms. Houses and streets were in straight lines, north to south.**

The reasons why the Inca city of Machu Picchu was abandoned are unknown. Lack of proper sanitation might have helped cause the spread of disease. The problem of sanitation and the difficulty of retaining a clean water supply when populations increase beyond a certain number limited the size of cities for centuries all over the world. The houses of Mohenjo-Daro (opposite) had bathrooms.

building materials by producing luxury goods like carvings and gold objects. When the Euphrates River changed its course, irrigation (watering systems) broke down. As the land dried up, it turned into unproductive desert. The city declined due to a lack of water and was then abandoned.

Settlements like Ur grew in areas that had useful features such as a supply of clean water, fuel (wood), and fertile land for crops. Whether a settlement becomes a city is ultimately decided by factors such as transportation routes and the distance to other settlements. In the beginning, however, water supplies are the most important consideration.

Early civilizations in the Americas—like those of the Aztec, Inca, and Maya—displayed what we would call city planning today. Temples and palaces were at the center of Incan cities, surrounded by large open areas. The rest of the city spread out from this central area. The closer a building was to the center, the more important it was. The same pattern can be seen in many modern cities.

Roman Maps

*As the Roman Empire began to expand from the fourth century **B.C.**, accurate maps were needed for planning settlements and recording land ownership.*

THE TASK OF MAPPING WAS GIVEN TO *AGRIMENSORES* (Roman land surveyors). These men had to produce detailed maps of property boundaries and buildings. Roman land surveyors also had to mark out surrounding territory to help plan further building.

The *groma* was the main instrument of the Roman land surveyor. It consisted of a long vertical staff topped by a horizontal metal cross. The cross was attached to the staff by a rod that allowed it to rotate freely. Attached to each arm was a lead weight, which acted as a plumb line. Since each weighed the same, the metal cross would always remain horizontal. The *groma* was designed to survey straight lines and right angles. That was done by placing the staff upright in the ground and "sighting" a distant object along the metal cross, which was kept level by the weights. So accurate was the *groma* that perfect squares could be marked out for the foundations of buildings.

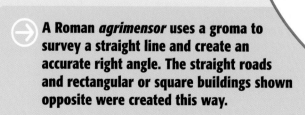

→ A Roman *agrimensor* uses a groma to survey a straight line and create an accurate right angle. The straight roads and rectangular or square buildings shown opposite were created this way.

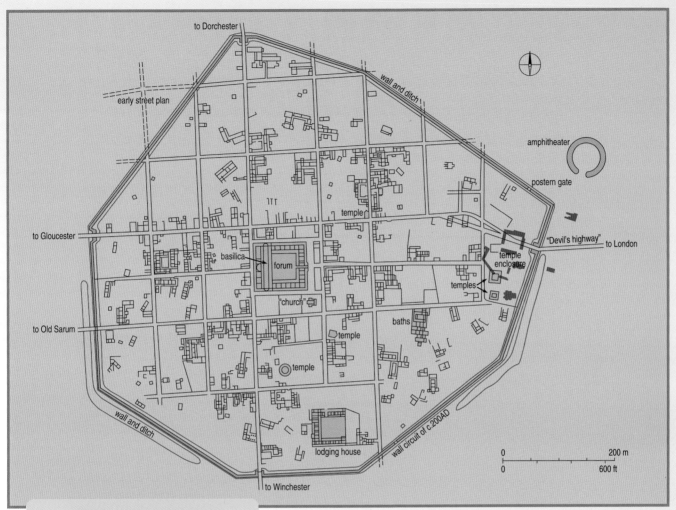

to Dorchester
early street plan
wall and ditch
amphitheater
postern gate
to Gloucester
basilica
forum
temple
"Devil's highway" to London
temple enclosure
temples
"church"
baths
to Old Sarum
temple
temple
wall and ditch
lodging house
wall circuit of c.200AD
to Winchester

0   200 m
0   600 ft

↑ **Silchester in southern England, built in the early third century, was a typical, carefully planned Roman settlement. The amphitheater, where games and dramas entertained the people, is outside the city walls.**

The *groma* was also used in the building of the famous Roman roads. Their routes are nearly always in straight lines. The *groma* was set up and another pole was put up in the distance. The *agrimensor* would sight along the *groma* and get the pole moved until it was in perfect alignment with all the earlier poles on the route. At the height of the Roman Empire, over 50,000 miles (80,000 km) of well-constructed highways had been built in Europe and North Africa.

Surveying and mapping skills were the backbone of Roman town planning. Maps showed land ownership and the value of land for taxation purposes. This is known as cadastral mapping. Romans favored a right-angle grid system for towns. Right angles made the movement of troops much easier, both within the city and for getting outside the city quickly.

East Asian Cities

The first maps in China and Japan were produced during the second century B.C. They were drawn for powerful governments that used them to control their empires.

MANY OF THE EARLIEST CHINESE MAPS USE A RECTANGULAR grid complete with a scale. China was always at the center of its own world maps, with "barbarians"—anyone who was not Chinese—put at the edges. In later centuries, settlements were mapped out in detail. Most urban maps were produced using little pictures to show the natural features and buildings of the area.

Many maps included detailed written information about the ownership or type of land and buildings being mapped. The maps were then used to tax the people and control land ownership.

In Japan, mapmaking was seen as the job of artists, not scientists or mathematicians. The result was the production of pictorial, panoramic maps. The pictures are easily recognizable—as temples or palaces, for example—and writing gives place names or building names and their uses. Different people could use the maps for different purposes. They might be used by a traveler, a general, or a government tax collector.

Maps of Japanese settlements became more accurate during the seventeenth century. The government ordered the production of new urban plans. They were carefully surveyed, drawn to scale, and accurately presented. The center of the town was shown in plan view, meaning that only the outlines of the buildings were drawn. In addition, the maps used symbols to show the different types of buildings. Symbols are sometimes hard to recognize, and often people prefer pictures. One solution was to draw the main town map as a flat plan and then add sketched pictures of the most important buildings.

The town was usually depicted within the surrounding countryside, with hills added in the distance to set the scene. Many of the maps were colored by hand. Most of them had a scale so the map user could work out rough distances. Fortifications were omitted from the maps to maintain secrecy.

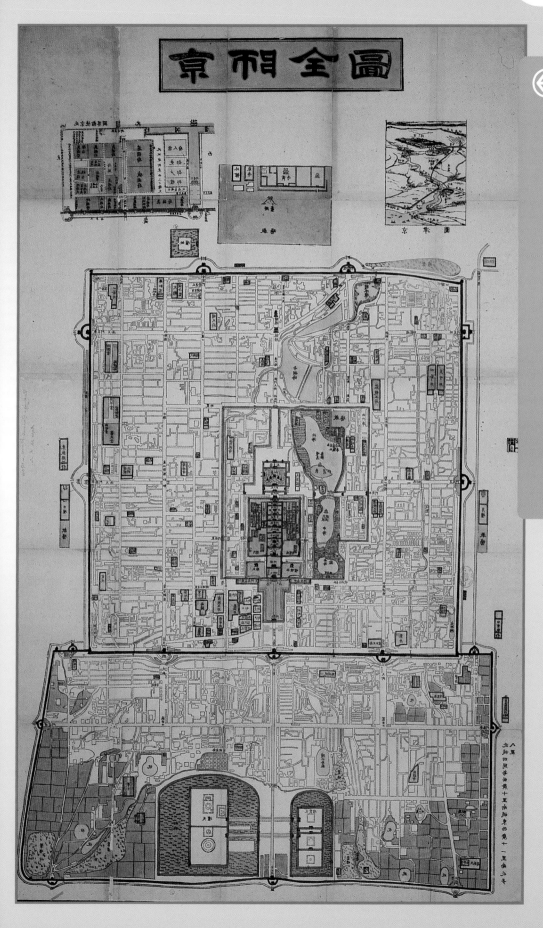

This Chinese map of Peking (Beijing) was produced using a woodcut template, probably around 1900. It shows the "Forbidden City," the 250-acre (1-sq-km) royal enclosure colored orange. Around it, marked with a pink border, is the Imperial City. The map is a mix of pictorial mapping and modern plan drawing. The top-left sketch shows Peking in relation to the Yellow Sea 100 miles (160 km) away. Twenty-four emperors lived in the Forbidden City, seldom leaving the grounds.

Early Modern Cities

Fourteenth- and fifteenth-century city maps were produced to help the traveler but also to promote the identity of the city. These maps were a kind of advert.

IN MEDIEVAL TIMES, ESPECIALLY IN ITALY, RULERS OF IMPORTANT settlements wanted maps to give them status. The result was a series of maps of city-states. City-states were cities that were rich and powerful enough to govern themselves. Cities like Venice and Florence were part of the country of Italy but they were not controlled by a central, national government. They raised their own taxes and had their own ruling families.

The city was at the center of these maps, and the agricultural land around had little detail. The maps emphasized the importance of the city to the surrounding area and showed the extensive area of countryside under the city's control.

As an important city-state that traded all across the known world, it is not surprising that Venice was a center of mapmaking. Venetian publishers produced maps of Italy and many maps of the world that were revised as new information was received from explorers. In the middle of the sixteenth century, the city-state of Rome became the birthplace of the atlas. Before then, maps had almost always been sold separately.

The Italian city of Imola drawn by Leonardo da Vinci. He divided the circle into eight segments to improve accuracy. This straight-down view is drawn to a more accurate scale than the oblique view on the opposite page.

A traditional oblique view of the Austrian city of Vienna. While the map presents the landmarks of the city in detail, important features cannot be seen, such as the river's path beyond the section visible in the foreground.

Leonardo da Vinci

Born in Tuscany in 1452, Leonardo da Vinci was a great painter, designer, and thinker. He used his skills to solve some of the problems with mapping that existed at that time. He worked on transforming what the eye could see into an accurate copy on paper.

Da Vinci improved many of the earlier fourteenth-century maps of Italian cities by drawing the urban area in the form of a plan. Instead of using small pictures for the buildings, he drew plans of the city layout and outlines of the buildings.

His maps moved away from the Italian tradition of pictorial oblique mapping, and toward outline plans. He included topographic detail, using shading to give the viewer a feel for the relief or shape of the land. Despite his improvements, city mapmakers continued to struggle with problems of scale and perspective.

The View From Above

Cartographers can either draw the city as they see it from ground level, or they can try to show a view from overhead.

FROM THE FOURTEENTH CENTURY ONWARD, MAPMAKERS used a combination of mapping, painting, sketching, and engraving to produce pictorial maps of a city. These panorama maps are artistic rather than scientific. To produce them, cartographers view the city from an elevated position, such as the top of a hill or high on a valley side, and draw what they can see. The result is an oblique view of the city and the surrounding land.

The panoramic map was drawn in perspective. This means that it was drawn as the artist saw the view. There were large buildings with a lot of detail sketched in the foreground and smaller representations of buildings in the background with little detail. Since the map was drawn from an oblique angle, it was not possible to draw the city to scale.

↓ **A view of Paris, France, from the top of the Eiffel Tower. In the late nineteenth-century, the invention of the hot air balloon and the construction of buildings like the Eiffel Tower gave cartographers a new perspective to work from when mapping cities.**

In the eighteenth century, the problems of perspective and variable scale led to survey-based maps. These were made by measuring distances on the ground.

In the nineteenth century, London was drawn in sections from a balloon tethered high above the city. Because of the wind, it was impossible to make sure that the balloon was always in the same place. However, the mapmaker could see the layout of the streets and roads for the first time.

A pictoral map of Little Rock, Arkansas, from 1871. Maps such as these were intended as decorative objects. The highlighted road layout and clearly visible landmarks would have made this map a usable, if not particularly practical, reference. In the late nineteenth century maps of towns and counties were very popular. To have one made gave a community a sense of importance—it put them on the map!

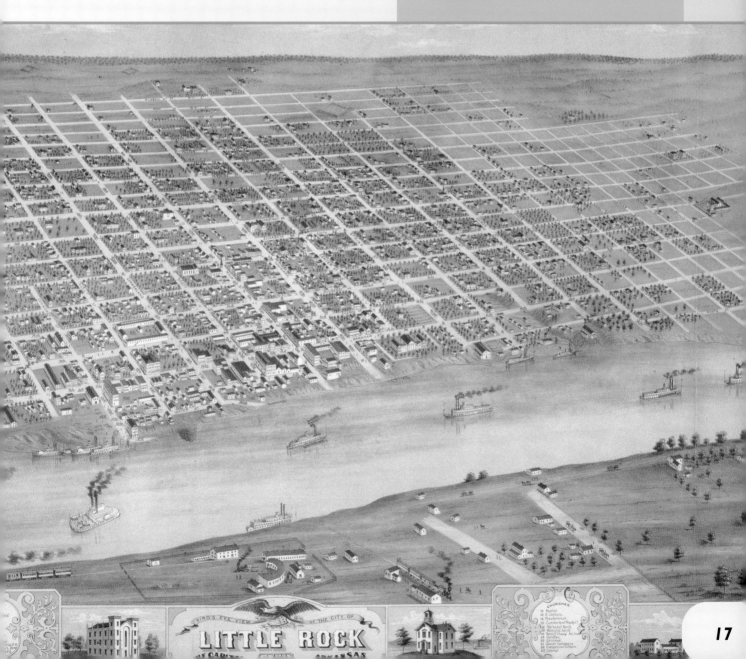

BIRD'S EYE VIEW OF THE CITY OF

LITTLE ROCK

Large-scale City Maps

The urban cartographer has to find ways of showing the structure of a city—its roads, buildings, and open spaces—to give people the information they need.

MODERN, PLANNED CITIES ARE VERY DIFFERENT FROM settlements that grow haphazardly. The city of Kano in the West African country of Nigeria, for example, has a population of well over a million. Like many African cities, it has attracted large numbers of migrants from the surrounding areas.

The city originally grew inside protective walls around the main market and mosque. Many of the inhabitants are packed into the old, unplanned housing of the city center constructed from mud bricks. All roads into the city converge in this central area, which also has the government buildings. Around the walled city newer

Chicago from an elevated viewpoint; an easy vantage point to find in a city of skyscrapers.

settlements developed in a similarly unplanned way. This zone of new development extends 30 to 60 miles (50 to 100 km) from the old city walls, and its complicated growth has caused problems for mapmakers.

Maps of Kano tend to be basic, with little detail of the external or internal structure of buildings. They have to be revised frequently since the shape and structure of the city change so often. The truth is, a map of Kano is never accurate because it is always out-of-date.

Up as Well as Out

A city where the layout has been planned is very different. The streets and buildings of Chicago, for example, are laid out in a regular pattern. The photograph at left shows an oblique aerial view of the city. You can identify the central business district area of the city by the tall buildings.

The mud huts of a city like Kano are all single story, so there is no need to map buildings internally. In Chicago, each floor of a skyscraper may have a different use. It is possible to map this using a variety of techniques.

Oblique mapping can help by "exploding" or cutting away the building and showing each floor by itself. The diagram shows a building that has been cut away to reveal the different uses for each floor.

fifth floor

fourth floor

third floor

second floor

A multilayer floorplan of the San Francisco Museum of Modern Art. Detailed floorplans allow the visitors to see what is on each level.

first floor

Nonexhibition space

Painting and sculpture collection

Californian art

Architecture and design

Photography and works on paper

Media arts

Special exhibitions and events

19

Height on Maps

Mapping a city on a flat piece of paper or presenting the map on a computer screen poses many problems.

HOW DO CARTOGRAPHERS show the heights of a city's tall buildings on a flat map? The answer goes back to the earliest pictorial maps of the Chinese and Japanese. Oblique sketches of buildings, carefully drawn, can show variation in height. This pictorial tradition is maintained in many modern city maps.

Oblique town maps today are drawn in ways that counteract the distortions of optical perspective. The cartographer does not just guess by looking at the city how big to draw the buildings, as in the early picture maps. Instead they follow scientific laws about how light reaches the eye from any viewpoint.

Axonometric Maps

One of the first cartographers to do this was an Austrian called Hermann Bollman. In addition to preparing oblique pictorial maps of valleys and mountainsides in winter for the tourist organizations in ski resorts, Bollman used his skills to draw city maps. By using an unusual type of perspective view, called an axonometric view, he developed a way of drawing each

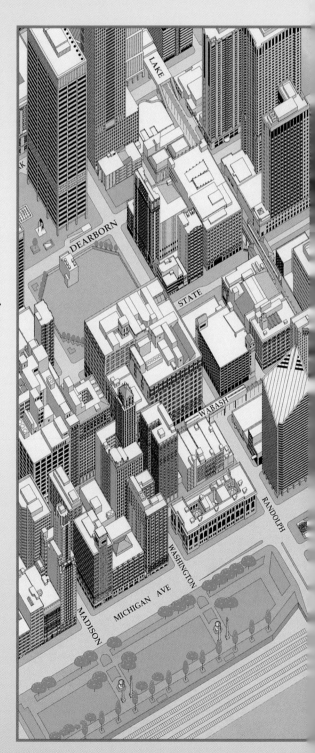

An axonometric computer-generated view of down-town Chicago. Major streets are broadened and named.

building in the city in great detail right across the map.

The buildings were all drawn on the same scale so the ones in the foreground are the same relative sizes as the ones in the background. The pictorial map views the city from a high oblique angle. Streets are drawn a little wider than they actually are to give the user a clear view of them and to allow for more detailed views of the buildings themselves. All major streets are named on the map to help the user.

Most of the maps produced by Bollman were of European cities, but he also applied his techniques to New York City, where the problem of representing tall buildings is at its most difficult. This illustration of Chicago (left) shows a computer-generated map in the Bollman style. The relative height of the buildings is clear. The key point about axonometric mapping is that it overcomes the problem of perspective. Buildings retain their relative size. However, such a map of the whole of Chicago at the scale shown here would be huge.

These maps can become more detailed. For example, buildings can be "split apart," and locations on each floor can be highlighted. If a computer generates these maps, often you can view them from different points in the city, or streets and buildings can be zoomed in on to see the detail. This is a long way from simple medieval picture maps!

Mapping Disease

In 1854, British physician Dr. John Snow discovered how cholera was transmitted. Maps were vital to both his investigation, and his efforts to prove the theory to others.

CHOLERA STILL KILLS THOUSANDS OF PEOPLE ALL OVER THE world every year. It causes stomach cramps, sickness, and diarrhea, and without medical treatment many victims die. In the nineteenth century nobody knew how to treat it effectively or to stop it from spreading!

In 1831, cholera reached Britain, having traveled with people who caught the disease in India. It was thought that the disease was spread through the air, but no attempts to clear the air had any effect. That year, 10,675 people died. A further epidemic hit London in August 1854. The worst affected areas were in the inner city, including Southwark, Lambeth, and most notably a very poor district called Soho.

During the first three days of September 1854, many people living on or near Broad Street, Soho, died. Every family in the area was affected. Those who were able to left the area quickly, leaving the poor and ill behind. By September 10, the death toll had passed 500.

→ **This illustration shows a typical slum area in nineteenth-century London. Overcrowding and unclean water provided perfect conditions for the spread of water-borne diseases such as cholera. Sewers ran directly into the Thames River, which supplied much of the drinking water supply.**

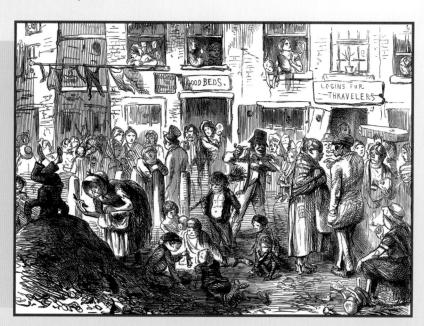

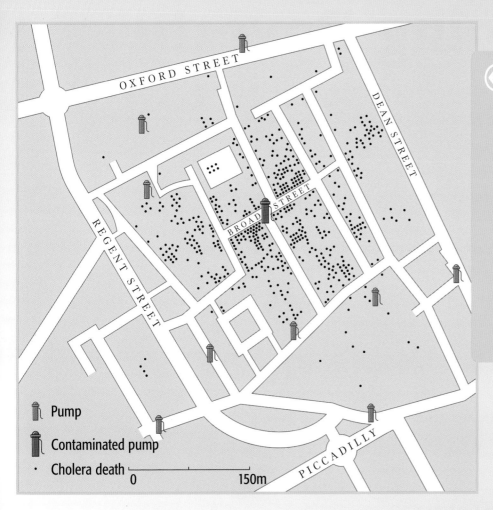

A reproduction of Dr. Snow's cholera map. The dots represent deaths from the disease. At the center is the Broad Street water pump. Despite the evidence of Snow's map, his theory was not believed until the Reverend Henry Whitehead helped Snow identify the original cause of the epidemic: Infected babies' diapers had been washed in water contained in a leaking cesspool just a few feet from the Broad Street water pump.

OXFORD STREET

DEAN STREET

BROAD STREET

REGENT STREET

PICCADILLY

Pump

Contaminated pump

Cholera death

0   150m

Dr. John Snow was the main reason that this number did not rise even higher. He had a practice in Soho and was eager to try and prove his theory that poor sanitation and infected water caused the spread of cholera. Snow interviewed all the affected families and plotted the location of deaths onto a base map of the area. By mapping the outbreaks of cholera, Snow was able to identify the center of the epidemic—a water pump on the corner of Broad Street and Cambridge Street, which was the main water supply for the Soho area.

The interviews he had conducted with the affected families all confirmed that this was their source of water. Examining water from the pump confirmed the source of infection, and his findings were passed on to the parish council. As an experiment, the pump handle was removed, making it impossible to draw water. The epidemic slowed down dramatically. Even so, by the end of September, 616 people had died in Soho.

Mapping Poverty

The statistical maps created by Charles Booth at the end of the nineteenth century would have an even greater effect on people's lives than Dr. Snow's cholera map.

CHARLES BOOTH WAS BORN IN LIVERPOOL, ENGLAND, in 1840. The son of a wealthy corn merchant, he joined his brothers to create the Booth Steamship Company. The company prospered, and he remained the company chairman until 1912. In the 1860s, Booth read the work of the French philosopher Auguste Comte, who suggested that industrialists should look after the welfare of workers and the poor. These ideas appealed to Booth, who was distressed by the poverty he saw around him.

Maps for Change

Booth was the first man to produce detailed maps of the living conditions and the social status of people at street level. He produced three maps covering all of London, each colored to show the different levels of poverty. His 1889 maps were published in a book called *Life and Labor of the People of London*.

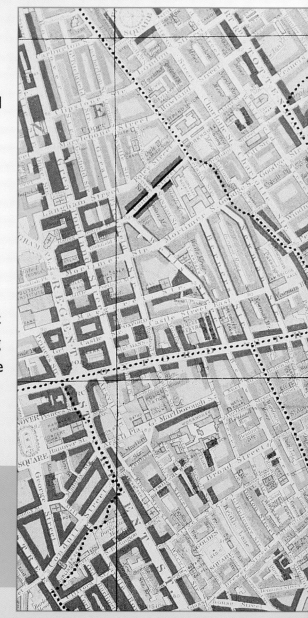

→ An example of Booth's statistical map; this is a relatively prosperous part of central London. The rich, grand squares are colored yellow. But a notorious slum area near Lincoln's Inn Fields is colored black.

He began his research in December 1886, and he continued until the middle of 1890. For every street in London he collected and recorded his data, coded it, and turned it into a color-coded map. He made observations of streets and consulted records of schools and charitable organizations. He recorded, in particular, details in his notebook about families with children. For each family he wrote their social class and their subcategory (one of eight per class).

Using this information, Booth took an average of the street's social class. He had a further eight categories to cover the mix of people living

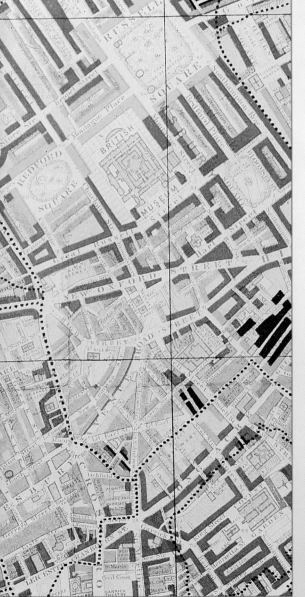

on the street and the physical condition of the street itself. Combining all this information, he placed each street in one of six color categories: black for the lowest social classes, red for the middle classes, and yellow for the upper-middle and upper classes.

Booth then plotted his data by hand onto an Ordnance Survey map of London. To make sure that his work was correct, Booth put his maps on display, inviting locals to correct the color coding if necessary.

Booth's maps, together with the work of others, provided evidence of the terrible living conditions of the poor in London. They showed that 30% of all people in the city were living in poverty. Booth strongly believed that if these people were given help, they could improve their lives.

Booth's work was not ignored. From 1905 to 1909 he was appointed a member of a royal commission set up to examine the poor law—legislation designed to help the needy. He urged the British government to introduce old-age pensions based on the findings of his studies. In 1908, they were introduced for all old people with income below a set level.

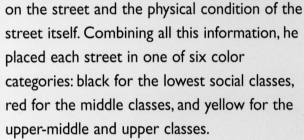

How Cities Grow

Geographical advantages—such as a good water supply and fertile soil for crops or grazing animals—are usually the starting point for the growth of a city.

MAPS GIVE VERY GOOD CLUES AS TO WHY SETTLEMENTS grew where they did. A map may show the original geographical factors that led to a site being chosen. Hundreds of years ago these factors were highly important.

The core areas of many cities (the part that was settled first) would almost always have been built on a dry site with a water supply nearby. Another major concern was often defense. High land or land inside a river bend allowed settlers to protect themselves. Areas of rich soil or lush pasture close to the settlement were important for the supply of food.

Paris through 2,000 years. The Romans (left) built on the south bank of the Seine River and the highly defensible Ile de La Cité. By the seventeenth century (below left) there were magnificent city squares and prestigious buildings. Today (below) almost all the Paris basin is urbanized.

Nearby building materials and fuel were also desirable. Usually there was a supply of wood, though some later settlements were located near a quarry. Coasts, lakes, and rivers all provided a supply of water and food, and were good for transportation and trading. If a settlement was located by a bridge over a river, it could control the crossing.

A map of most settlements shows a network of roads and railways radiating out from the center. Cities that display such a pattern are known as route centers or nodal points.

The more favorable factors a place had, the more attractive it became for settlement, and the quicker it grew. Over time these factors became less important than the settlement's position in relation to other settlements. Being close to other settlements and having good transportation access to them would result in growth through trade.

Successful settlements grow and develop

➔ **Examples of favorable location factors. Many settlements' first priority was defense and it could be made easier by an area's topography. For most of the big cities in the world–those that are not modern, planned cities–original positive location factors can be identified. The name of the city of Koblenz comes from the Latin word for confluence, *confluentes*.**

Confluence of two rivers
Protected on two or three sides by water. Koblenz, Germany; Lyons, France.

River crossing
Narrow point in a valley or shallow part of a river allows a crossing point. Kansas City.

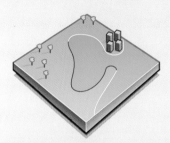

Natural harbor
Gives protection; encourages trade without much harbor investment. New York City.

Margin or head of delta
A plentiful supply of water and fertile alluvial soil attract settlers. Cairo, Egypt.

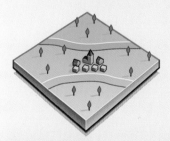

Portage point
Goods are transferred to and from road or rail and boats. Chicago (on Lake Michigan).

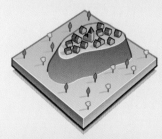

Defensive hilltop site
Easily defended and with clear view of surrounding area. Athens, Greece.

Offshore island
Easily defended, and sea trade routes around them can be controlled. Venice.

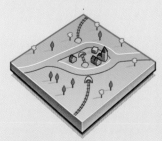

Island in a river or bay
Similarly defensible; passage across is controlled. Ile de La Cité, Paris.

Pittsburgh is the city that gave the world the polio vaccine. It is also the location of the first petroleum refinery and the first movie house.

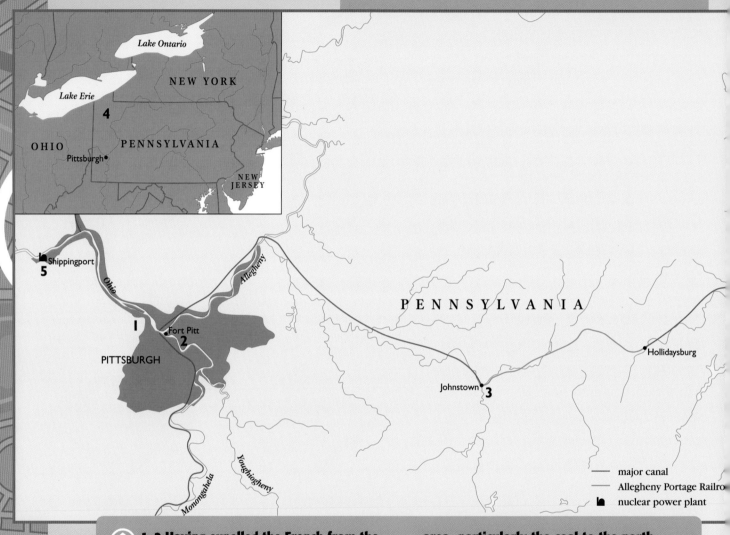

Lake Ontario

NEW YORK

Lake Erie

4

OHIO   PENNSYLVANIA

Pittsburgh•

NEW JERSEY

Shippingport
5

Ohio

Allegheny

PENNSYLVANIA

1

Fort Pitt
2

PITTSBURGH

Hollidaysburg

Johnstown•
3

Monongahela

Youghiogheny

—— major canal
—— Allegheny Portage Railro
⬛ nuclear power plant

1, 2 Having expelled the French from the area, the British built the fort in 1761 to ensure dominance at the source of the Ohio River. The fort offered security to early settlers against the Native American tribes. After the Revolutionary War, Pittsburgh became an outfitting point for settlers traveling west down the Ohio.
3, 4 The Pennsylvania Canal and the Allegheny Portage Railroad were both completed in 1834. They opened up markets for trade and shipping, and ensured that the mineral wealth of the area—particularly the coal to the north—could be exploited to make iron and steel. The billionaire steel magnate Andrew Carnegie built his industrial empire in Pittsburgh, creating thousands of jobs.
5 The world's first full-scale nuclear power plant for the production of electricity was opened here in 1957. The plant was viable because of the power requirements of Pittsburgh, and the city profited from the new energy resource, not least through a reduction in smoke pollution.

their own functions separate from their neighboring towns and cities. The functions of a city are its economic and social activities. Towns and cities can often be classified by their main function.

Settlement Functions

Most large cities actually have many functions, and it is possible to identify them from maps. City functions include: (1) Commercial—retail parks and major shopping centers; (2) Industrial—heavy industry, high-tech industry, and business parks; (3) Residential—housing for the population; (4) Service—medical care, schools, and universities; (5) Financial—banking and finance center; (6) Entertainment—cultural attractions, theaters, theme parks, and leisure facilities; (7) Government—representative bodies (councils, senates, and the like), tax offices, police, law courts.

Today, the factors for the location and growth of cities are mainly economic and political. Site factors are less important since many of them can now be controlled. Rivers can be straightened, tunnels can be built through hills, and bridges span rivers and valleys. All of these changes to the urban scene are examples of overcoming negative site factors.

Town and Country
People live in one of two main areas: rural—small settlements or individual farms in the countryside—or urban—in a town or city. People who move from rural areas to cities (mainly to find work) are known as rural–urban migrants. Cities perform functions that give people the opportunity to work in a variety of jobs. But in rich countries many people are moving from urban areas to the countryside in search of a better quality of life. They want more space, less noise and pollution. Millions now commute into cities to work each day, which requires transportation networks with capacities undreamt of fifty years ago.

An example of a city that grew because of political decisions is Washington, D.C. It became the U.S. capital shortly after the Revolutionary War because it was at the center of the original 13 states of the Union. To make any other city the capital would have caused arguments among the states.

The city is at the head of the Potomac River, which was certainly a good site factor for communications. Later, people began to realize that building in a swampy area led to the spread of sickness and disease in the summer months. If Washington, D.C., had not been made the capital—bringing thousands of government jobs and encouraging places like theaters and museums to open up and be successful—negative site factors would have restricted the growth of the city.

Planning New Towns

As cities develop, attractive new buildings are constructed on the outskirts, and buildings in the center often become neglected and overcrowded.

During the industrial revolution in the nineteenth century, many cities throughout the world experienced problems with overcrowding and poor living conditions. People who came to the city to work often ended up living in unsafe and unsanitary slums.

Ebenezer Howard was a British town planner who had worked in London and Chicago. He was concerned about the living conditions of working-class people in city centers. In 1902, he published a book called *Garden Cities of Tomorrow*. Howard proposed creating new towns to house the people living in these poor areas. The towns would be well planned, with houses laid out in traffic-free streets and large amounts of open space. He believed that there should be a maximum number of people (30,000) allowed to live in these new towns to avoid overcrowding.

The idea of the garden city was to provide people with a better quality of life, but without completely

THE THREE MAGNETS

Ebenezer Howard's "3 magnets of attraction," drawn in 1902 to show the pluses and minuses of living in different places. Howard wanted to persuade people that "Town-Country" was the most attractive option.

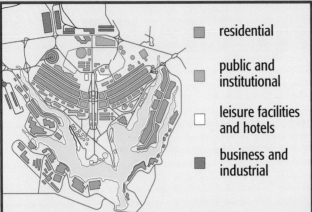

- **residential**
- **public and institutional**
- **leisure facilities and hotels**
- **business and industrial**

A map and aerial photograph of Brasilia. Only a newly planned city could have such a regular and symmetrical layout. Each block in the photograph houses 2,500 people. What do you think it is like to live in one of those blocks?

losing the comforts of the city. People would still have jobs, but would live in new homes in pleasant surroundings. By building the garden cities on cheap agricultural land outside the main city, Howard wanted to bring the countryside to the towns. He was able to persuade government and business to act on his ideas, and two garden cities were built in England during his lifetime. Howard's ideas influenced city planning throughout the world.

Brasilia: A South American New Town

In 1956, the Brazilian government chose the site for the new town of Brasilia. The layout of the city was planned to look from above like an airplane or bird. The two "wings" were for housing. The central section was zoned into areas for hotels, commerce, local government, national government, and culture. Leisure parks and open grasslands would surround the city. The government moved to its new location in 1960.

Land Use in Cities

Cities change as time passes. They get bigger (and very few get smaller). But that is not the only change. What happens in different parts of the city also changes.

AN AREA OF THE CITY THAT USED TO BE A BUSY INDUSTRIAL site a few decades ago might today be full of expensive luxury apartments—or it might be a wasteland. These changes can be mapped.

Different parts of a city have different activities in them. City maps reveal residential areas, retail parks, schools, and recreational open spaces. Often certain functions, such as industrial production, are in areas that are separate from the rest of the city.

If you drew a line (called a transect) from a city center on a map to the outskirts, you would see a number of changes in land use along it. By studying and mapping urban structure in many cities, models are developed that try to explain the land use patterns and give us an understanding of the economic and social processes that give them their shape.

Burgess found that Chicago in the 1920s followed the same pattern as Manchester, described 60 years earlier, but without the factory zone. The different zones are not circular because the city is on Lake Michigan.

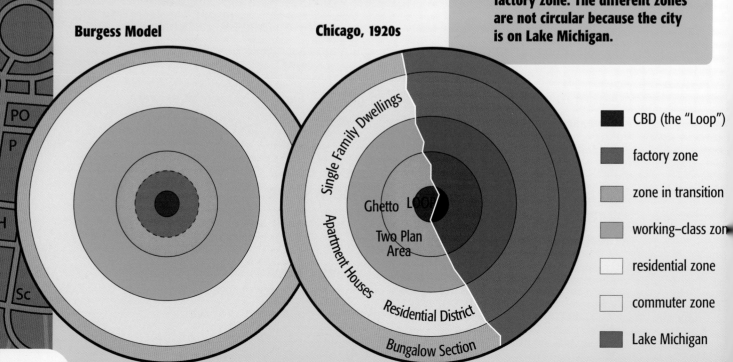

Burgess Model

Chicago, 1920s

Single Family Dwellings

Apartment Houses

Ghetto   LOOP

Two Plan Area

Residential District

Bungalow Section

- CBD (the "Loop")
- factory zone
- zone in transition
- working–class zon
- residential zone
- commuter zone
- Lake Michigan

An Early Land Use Theory

During the 1840s, the German philosopher Friedrich Engels wrote a book called *The Condition of the Working Classes in England.* The book was based on his experiences living and working in Manchester, which was a fast-growing city full of slum housing and factories. Engels described not only the conditions of factory workers but also how the city was organized.

In the 1920s, a teacher at the University of Chicago, Ernest W. Burgess, read Engels' book and compared what Engels had found in Manchester to the situation in Chicago. Burgess found repeated patterns of land use. He developed a theory that described what happened to land not just in one city, but in many cities. This theory is now called the Burgess "Concentric Zone Model."

The Burgess Model

The concentric model presents a series of rings, each of which comprises a different type of land use. The middle of the rings is the central area, known as the "central business district" (CBD). In this area there are department stores, large banks, offices, entertainment (bars, theaters, movie theaters), a variety of shops, and good transportation facilities. Land prices are high because it is desirable for businesses to locate there.

The City of Sunderland

The maps of Sunderland (a city in northeast England) show changing land use from 1971 to 1996. The built-up areas of the city expand into areas that were once agricultural land. The maps show the increasing need for new housing. The original concentration of housing and roads near the coast was built when Sunderland was an important center of shipbuilding and heavy industry. This industry has declined since the 1970s. The central business district is located to the south of the river. The best housing is located to the very south of the city away from the industry. The old, poorer housing is located next to the river, where the old industry was located. New housing is to the west. The city has followed the Burgess model in several ways, but the locations of the sea and the river have distorted the ring pattern.

→ Land use 1971; most housing is close to the docks.

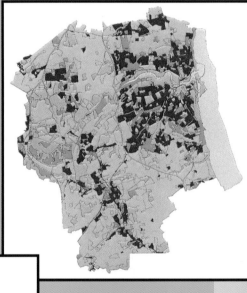

↓ Land use 1996; farm-land becomes residential and urban green area.

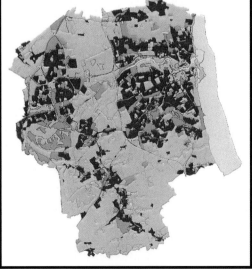

■ woodland, natural areas

■ urban green areas

■ industry, commerce, transportation

■ residential

□ agriculture

□ water

Around the CBD is the "zone in transition." Land use here is mixed. The area may be run down and have poor transportation networks. This part of the city is less desirable for large stores and other facilities. It consists mainly of older and overcrowded housing along with less impressive offices, plus warehouses and some small-scale industry. Housing is usually quite cheap because of its low quality, so poor people live there. Ethnic minorities sometimes make up the bulk of the population.

The "zone of working men's homes" contains housing built for people who have moved out of the zone in transition. The people living there have relatively low rents and an effective transportation network to get to work. All cities grow outward as housing and transportation develop side-by-side.

The "residential zone" is an area of higher-quality housing for wealthier city dwellers. Houses are larger, and there is more open space. Housing is low density—there are fewer houses per unit of land. In modern cities, these

The high-rise apartment blocks of the Bronx, New York. Millions of dollars were spent improving housing in the area during the 1940s, but by the 1980s whole neighborhoods were left mostly abandoned.

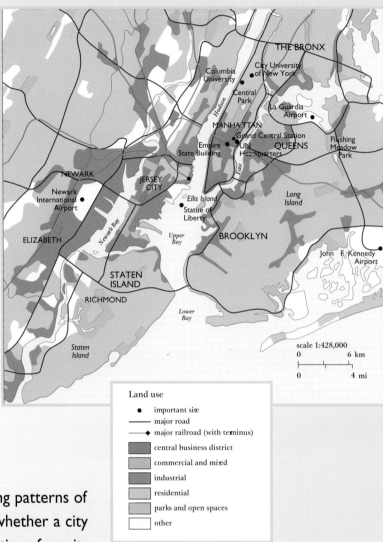

A map of land use in New York City. The Bronx is on the New York state mainland.

areas have retail parks and office developments mixed with housing.

The "commuter zone" is the area beyond the edge of the city. Land use there has changed from farmland to housing and leisure facilities. The urban area eats into the surrounding countryside. High rates of car ownership have allowed this growth, and the residents can take advantage of this and the cheaper cost of land to live on bigger properties.

Thematic Maps

Maps are the ideal way of showing changing patterns of land use over time. They can help us see whether a city follows the Burgess model, has slight variations from it, or has grown in a completely different way.

Maps can show the true character of cities by mapping features other than buildings and space. Mapping of statistics, such as income levels, reveals areas of poverty and areas in need of new development. Armed with a detailed set of these thematic maps, city planners can identify and tackle urban problems.

New York City's planners, for example, have tried to solve the problems of poor housing and deprived neighborhoods in two ways. First, they have encouraged new growth at the city edge. This has meant building on much of the open space around the city. The second method has been to improve things in the city center to encourage people to stay. The planners have tried to regenerate open spaces and improve leisure or recreation facilities.

Land use

- important site
— major road
—◆ major railroad (with terminus)
central business district
commercial and mixed
industrial
residential
parks and open spaces
other

scale 1:428,000

0   6 km

0   4 mi

Mass Transportation

The most important feature of a map showing the city's public transportation system is not the distance from one place to another, but where to get on and off.

THE EFFICIENCY OF CITIES THAT HAVE millions of commuters and visitors relies heavily on clear mapping of public transportation.

The usual solution is to create a topological subway map. This type of mapping is really like an electrical circuit diagram because, like the diagram, it does not show things to scale, and it uses symbols. The most important facts to show are the positions of subway

A topological map of the London underground. This map is designed for clarity and user-friendliness. Station locations on the map do not relate to each other in the same way that they do in reality.

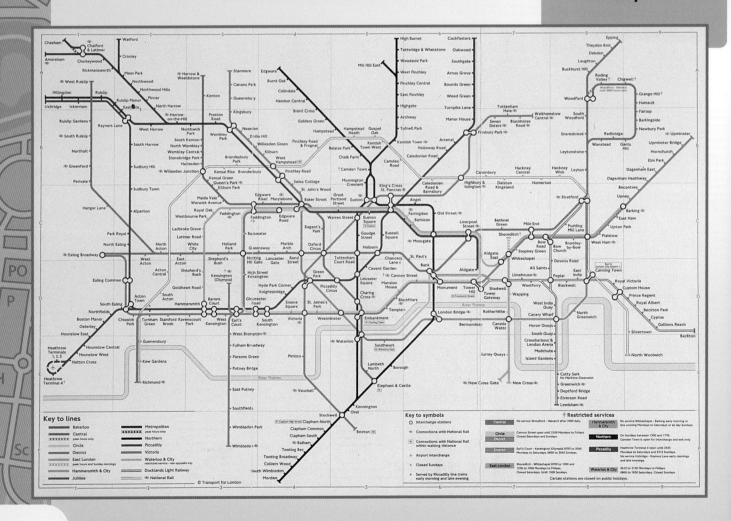

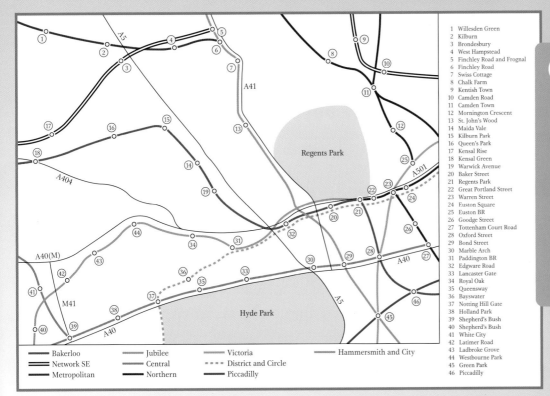

1	Willesden Green
2	Kilburn
3	Brondesbury
4	West Hampstead
5	Finchley Road and Frognal
6	Finchley Road
7	Swiss Cottage
8	Chalk Farm
9	Kentish Town
10	Camden Road
11	Camden Town
12	Mornington Crescent
13	St. John's Wood
14	Maida Vale
15	Kilburn Park
16	Queen's Park
17	Kensal Rise
18	Kensal Green
19	Warwick Avenue
20	Baker Street
21	Regents Park
22	Great Portland Street
23	Warren Street
24	Euston Square
25	Euston BR
26	Goodge Street
27	Tottenham Court Road
28	Oxford Street
29	Bond Street
30	Marble Arch
31	Paddington BR
32	Edgware Road
33	Lancaster Gate
34	Royal Oak
35	Queensway
36	Bayswater
37	Notting Hill Gate
38	Holland Park
39	Shepherd's Bush
40	Shepherd's Bush
41	White City
42	Latimer Road
43	Ladbroke Grove
44	Westbourne Park
45	Green Park
46	Piccadilly

Legend:
— Bakerloo
— Jubilee
— Victoria
— Hammersmith and City
— Network SE
— Central
··· District and Circle
— Metropolitan
— Northern
— Piccadilly

A topographic map of actual station locations for a section of the map on page 36. Information about features on the surface–roads and parks–is included. Follow the different rail lines to locate the same stations on both maps.

stations relative to each other. In New York, the Fifth Avenue Station is the stop between Times Square Station and Grand Central Station. That is what the traveler needs to know. The true distance between each of the stations is not really important. So subway maps are not drawn true to scale, but instead they stretch and reduce distances to make the map more readable and more compact.

The map to the left is part of the topological underground railway map of London (the subway in London is called "the underground" or "the tube"). The map shows the underground lines and the location of the stations. The tracks are drawn as straight lines with few curves, and the whole system is shown on one map that can fit inside your pocket. The central area of the map is stretched, while the distances between stations in the suburbs look much shorter than they really are. The real tracks are not straight lines, and they sometimes go uphill and downhill. The map above shows the accurate, to-scale location of some of the stations and track direction.

This idea of simplifying the routes of subways has been extended to all forms of transportation. Many bus maps also use topological mapping techniques.

Tourist Guides

The tourist map is a specialized form of mapping that helps someone who has never been to the city find their way around it.

TOURIST CARTOGRAPHERS HAVE TO DECIDE WHAT FEATURES to include to make the map "user-friendly." A good starting point is to make the streets on the map wider than they actually are. This lets the mapmaker add details like road names, transportation routes, and landmarks more clearly. Using sketches of some individual buildings allows map readers to find out where they are by recognizing what is around them.

The map may also help in finding locations by supplying lettered and numbered grid squares. A list of places and streets, known as a gazetteer, lists the grid references for the most popular destinations. At popular tourist sites, a large poster version of the tourist map can often be found on a noticeboard, with a "YOU ARE HERE" arrow. It lets the visitors orient themselves with their surroundings. As with most kinds of map—including pictorial maps, panoramic maps, and axonometric maps—knowing where you are on the map is the first step to using it.

A tourist consults a map outside the Reichstag in Berlin. Important landmarks like this one are often illustrated as well as marked on the map.

New Technology

When finding your way in the city, you no longer have to take a paper map with you. Maps are available from in-car navigation systems, through palm PCs, and cellphones. Early in-car navigation systems relied on CDs that held information about an area in the form of a map. Today, Global Positioning System (GPS) satellites can locate your car's position. The computer software is even able to give a "best guess" of position if the car cannot receive the GPS signal—in a narrow city street or in a tunnel, for example. The type of map provided by these systems is similar to a tourist map because it shows a simplified street pattern, highlights important landmarks, and only includes the most vital information for navigation.

A GPS-based in-car navigation system. These devices give the user directions to their destination using an onboard map and a GPS receiver that gives their vehicle's current location.

For the tourist, as well as route planners, most navigation computer software allows you to select further information that you want to include on your map. It could include accommodations, tourist attractions, landmarks, or detailed route plan notes.

Are These Maps Really New?

These maps are actually an updated electronic version of old route maps. Coaching maps (showing the routes of horse-drawn carriages that you could catch just like a bus) were produced for the seventeenth-century traveler. They only included the road and features on either side that you could see from the road. The maps were sometimes produced on thin strips of paper that could be unwound and read like a scroll. The maps included distances between places, important road junctions, and landmarks. The aims of the seventeenth-century mapmaker and the GPS cartographer are the same—to give travelers only as much information as they need—but the way of delivering that information is very different.

Glossary

Words in *italics* have their own entries in the glossary.

aerial photograph (or air photograph) – a photograph looking straight down at Earth

agrimensores – Roman land surveyors who worked in the towns and on military campaigns throughout the Roman Empire

axonometric maps – maps showing three-dimensional objects so that the scale for each object is the same whether close up or in the distance. Building heights, for example, can be compared right across the area mapped; this cannot be done with the alternative display method, *perspective* viewing, in which objects appear smaller the farther away they are.

Aztecs – a people who in the 15th and early 16th century ruled a large empire in what is now central and southern Mexico. They probably came from the northern Mexico plateau in the 12th century.

base map – a map that shows base data, fundamental cartographic information such as political boundaries and topography (See topographic map)

bearing – the direction someone is heading measured as an angle away from north. Due north has a bearing of 0 degrees, while due west has a bearing of 270 degrees. Bearing is also sometimes used to describe angular position or direction in relation to any two known points.

cadastral system – a method of recording ownership of land based on registers, legal documents, and maps showing the boundaries of individual tracts

cartography – the task of collecting information and producing maps. People who do this are called cartographers

An aerial photograph of the crowds gathered for the inauguration of President Barack Obama in January 2009. This picture was taken from an aircraft flying below cloud-level for a better view.

The magnetic compass was first used for navigation in China around 1,000 years ago. It is still an important navigational tool although it is rarely used for long-distance navigation anymore.

CBD – the "central business district" of a large city where commerce, government, and other important activities take place

cesspool – a covered underground tank or well for the collection of waste matter and water, especially sewage

cholera – a water-borne disease. Symptoms include sickness and diarrhea, which can lead to death if untreated

city-state – a city powerful and rich enough to run its own affairs more or less independent of a central national government. Ancient city-states such as Athens and city-states of the Middle Ages such as Venice were like small countries.

commuters – workers who live some distance away from their place of work and must use transportation systems such as railways and buses, or their cars, every working day

compass – an instrument showing the direction of *magnetic north* using a magnetic needle. *Bearing* can be calculated by using a compass.

concentric – describes a series of circles one inside the other focused on the same point

delta – the area at the mouth of some rivers where the main stream breaks up into smaller rivulets

favelas – a settlement of shacks or semipermanent shelters lying on the

outskirts of a city, usually in South America (*see also* squatter settlements)

Forbidden City – The imperial palace within the inner city of Beijing, China. The 9,000 rooms inside housed the emperor and imperial court from 1421 to 1911. It was called the Forbidden City because no commoner or foreigner could enter without permission from court officials.

fortifications – structures, such as walls, built to strengthen a place's defenses

functions – the different aspects of a city that make it work; the services offered by an urban settlement, including opportunities for work, entertainment, investment, or shelter

gazetteer – a list of names of places, with location specified, often accompanied by a map

Global Positioning System (GPS) – a system of 24 satellites orbiting Earth and sending out highly accurate radio signals indicating where they are. A GPS receiver held by someone on Earth can interpret the signals and calculate the receiver's position on Earth.

grid system – a mesh of horizontal and vertical lines over the face of a map to pinpoint the position of places. The mesh of lines often helps show distance of locations east and north from a set position. The zero point can be any convenient location and is often the bottom-left corner of the map.

groma – a land-surveying instrument used by Roman *agrimensores* to set out right angles on the ground

The Inca city of Machu Picchu. The Inca built many of these hilltop cities, linking them with an extensive road network.

Incas – South American Indians who ruled an empire along the Pacific coast and in the Andean Highlands at the time of the Spanish conquest in 1532. They built a vast network of roads throughout their empire, and their architecture was advanced. They kept no written records. Machu Picchu in the Andes Mountains of south-central Peru is one of their fortress cities.

Industrial Revolution – the period of history (in the late 18th and 19th centuries) when some societies that had been mainly agricultural were transformed into manufacturing economies, using coal and steam power to run factories and transport goods

land use – how human beings use land, for example, for housing, agriculture, or recreation. Land use is different from land cover, which describes the natural vegetation or environment in an area, for example, forest, desert, or ice cap.

leisure – time during which somebody has no obligations or work responsibilities, and therefore is free to engage in enjoyable activities

low density – density is an expression of the number of items per unit area. For example, a low-density housing area would mean that there are fewer houses per unit of land than in a built-up area.

magnate – one who has a lot of wealth and power, especially someone in business or industry

magnetic north – the northerly direction in Earth's magnetic field, indicated by the direction in which a compass needle points

Mayans – a people who created a vast and sophisticated civilization in what is now southern Mexico, Guatemala, and northern Belize. At its height, from about 250 A.D. to 900 A.D., Mayan culture created more than 40 cities with populations ranging from 5,000 to 50,000. The Mayans built huge stone buildings and pyramid temples, and—unlike the *Incas*—had a written language.

Mesopotamia – ancient region located between the Tigris and Euphrates rivers in modern Iraq and Syria. It was the site of several early urban civilizations.

oblique view – a view of Earth's surface from above, not looking straight down but at an angle to the surface

optical perspective – geometrical scientific laws about how light reaches the eye from any viewpoint; followed when making *oblique* maps (*see also* perspective)

The effects of optical perspective are a problem for mapmakers. A map of Chicago drawn from this viewpoint, for example, would make features near to the shore appear much larger than similar features inland.

panorama – a wide *oblique* view, showing an area of countryside or the extent of a city

pension – a fixed amount of money paid regularly to somebody during retirement by the government, a former employer, or an insurance company

perspective – a method of showing three-dimensional objects graphically in such a way that they look natural, as they would in the real world. Objects appear smaller the farther away they are.

pictorial map – a map that uses small pictures to represent buildings and other important landmarks

portage – the carrying of small boats or their cargo overland between two navigable waterways

A squatter settlement (*favela*) in Rio de Janeiro, Brazil. Semipermanent settlements like this one develop organically, with no planned structure. They often lack basic amenities like electricity or running water.

relief – the shape of Earth's surface, its hills, mountains, and depressions

sanitation – protection of health through hygiene, preventing infections and epidemics

scale – the ratio of the size of a map to the area of the real world that it represents

situation – a settlement's location in relation to the surrounding land and features and other settlements

slum – an overcrowded area of a city in which the housing is typically in very bad condition

squatter settlements – informal areas of housing, like *favelas*, on the edge of many third-world cities. People who have moved from other places, often the countryside, gather there to settle.

template – something that serves as a pattern from which other similar things can be made

topographic map – a map that shows natural features such as hills, rivers, and forests, and man-made features such as roads and buildings

topological maps – maps that show relationships among objects but are not necessarily to scale like a *topographic map*. A topological subway map, for example, shows the sequence of the stations–their relationship along the railroad line–but not the actual distances between them.

transect – a line drawn across an area or a map that is used to sample varying characteristics, such as land use

urban – describes built-up areas of human settlement; towns and cities

urbanization – the growth of a settlement so that it gradually comes to resemble a town or city

Further Reading and Web Sites

Aczel, Amir D. *The Riddle of the Compass: The Invention That Changed the World*. New York: Harcourt, 2001.

Arnold, Caroline. *The Geography Book: Activities for Exploring, Mapping, and Enjoying Your World*. New York: Wiley, 2002.

Barber, Peter, and April Carlucci, eds. *The Lie of the Land*. London: British Library Publications, 2001.

Brown, Carron, ed. *The Best-Ever Book of Exploration*. New York: Kingfisher Books, 2002.

Davis, Graham. *Make Your Own Maps*. New York: Sterling, 2008.

Deboo, Ana. *Mapping the Seas and Skies*. Chicago: Heinemann-Raintree, 2007.

Dickinson, Rachel. *Tools of Navigation: A Kid's Guide to the History & Science of Finding Your Way*. White River Junction, VT: Nomad Press, 2005.

Doak, Robin S. *Christopher Columbus: Explorer of the New World*. Minneapolis, MN: Compass Point Books, 2005.

Ehrenberg, Ralph E. *Mapping the World: An Illustrated History of Cartography*. Washington, D.C.: National Geographic, 2005.

Field, Paula, ed. *The Kingfisher Student Atlas of North America*. Boston: Kingfisher, 2005.

Ganeri, Anita, and Andrea Mills. *Atlas of Exploration*. New York: DK Publishing, 2008.

Graham, Alma, ed. *Discovering Maps*. Maplewood, NJ: Hammond World Atlas Corporation, 2004.

Harvey, Miles. *The Island of Lost Maps: A True Story of Cartographic Crime*. New York: Random House, 2000.

Harwood, Jeremy. *To the Ends of the Earth: 100 Maps That Changed the World*. Newton Abbot, United Kingdom: David and Charles, 2006.

Haywood, John. *Atlas of World History*. New York: Barnes and Noble, 1997.

Hazen, Walter A. *Everyday Life: Exploration & Discovery*. Tuscon, AZ: Good Year Books, 2005.

Henzel, Cynthia Kennedy. *Mapping History*. Edina, MN: Abdo Publishing, 2008.

Jacobs, Frank. *Strange Maps: An Atlas of Cartographic Curiosities*. New York: Viking Studio, 2009.

Keay, John. *The Great Arc: The Dramatic Tale of How India Was Mapped and Everest Was Named*. New York: HarperCollins, 2000.

Levy, Janey. *Mapping America's Westward Expansion: Applying Geographic Tools And Interpreting Maps*. New York: Rosen Publishing, 2005.

Levy, Janey. *The Silk Road: Using a Map Scale to Measure Distances*. New York: PowerKids Press, 2005.

McDonnell, Mark D. *Maps on File*. New York: Facts on File, 2007.

McNeese, Tim. *Christopher Columbus and the Discovery of the Americas*. Philadelphia: Chelsea House, 2006.

Mitchell, Robert, and Donald Prickel. *Contemporary's Number Power: Graphs, Tables, Schedules, and Maps*. Lincolnwood, IL: Contemporary Books, 2000.

Oleksy, Walter G. *Mapping the Seas*. New York: Franklin Watts, 2003.

Oleksy, Walter G. *Mapping the Skies*. New York: Franklin Watts, 2003.

Resnick, Abraham. *Maps Tell Stories Too: Geographic Connections to American History*. Bloomington, IN: IUniverse, 2002.

Rirdan, Daniel. *Wide Ranging World Map*. Phoenix, AZ: Exploration, 2002.

Ross, Val. *The Road to There: Mapmakers and Their Stories*. Toronto, Canada: Tundra Books, 2009.

Rumsey, David, and Edith M. Punt. *Cartographica Extraordinaire: The Historical Map Transformed.* Redlands, CA: Esri Press, 2004.

Short, Charles Rennie. *The World through Maps.* Buffalo, NY: Firefly Books, 2003.

Smith, A. G. *Where Am I? The Story of Maps and Navigation.* Toronto, Canada: Fitzhenry and Whiteside, 2001.

Taylor, Barbara. *Looking at Maps.* North Mankato, MN: Franklin Watts, 2007.

Taylor, Barbara. *Maps and Mapping.* New York: Kingfisher, 2002.

Virga, Vincent. *Cartographia: Mapping Civilizations.* London: Little, Brown and Company, 2007.

Wilkinson, Philip. *The World of Exploration.* New York: Kingfisher, 2006.

Wilson, Patrick. *Navigation and Signalling.* Broomall, PA: Mason Crest Publishers, 2002.

Winchester, Simon. *The Map That Changed the World: William Smith and the Birth of Modern Geology.* New York: HarperCollins, 2001.

Zuravicky, Orli. *Map Math: Learning About Latitude and Longitude Using Coordinate Systems.* New York: PowerKids Press, 2005.

Online Resources

www.davidrumsey.com
The David Rumsey map collection. This online library contains around 20,000 historical and modern maps.

http://dma.jrc.it
The mapping collection of the European Commission Joint Research Center. Includes ineractive maps as well as maps documenting environmental and human disasters around the world.

http://etc.usf.edu/Maps/
The University of South Florida's online mapping library. The collection includes historical and modern maps from around the world.

www.lib.utexas.edu/maps
The University of Texas's online map library. The collection includes old CIA maps, historical maps, and thematic maps from around the world.

www2.lib.virginia.edu/exhibits/lewis_clark
An online exhibition at the University of Virginia with information on historic expeditions, including Lewis and Clark.

http://maps.google.com
Google's online mapping resource, includes conventional maps and satellite images for most of the world, as well as street-level photography of Western urban centers.

http://maps.nationalgeographic.com
National Geographic's online mapping service.

http://memory.loc.gov/ammem/gmdhtml/
Map collections from 1500–1999 at the Library of Congress. The collection includes maps made by early explorers, maps of military campaigns, and thematic maps on a variety of topics.

www.nationalatlas.gov
Online national atlas for the United States. Includes customizable topographic maps on a range of different themes.

http://strangemaps.wordpress.com
A frequently updated collection of unusual maps, from maps of imaginary lands to creative ways of displaying data in map form.

www.unc.edu/awmc/mapsforstudents.html
A large collection of free maps, covering many different subjects and regions, hosted by the University of North Carolina.

www.un.org/Depts/Cartographic/
    english/htmain.htm
United Nations mapping agency website. contains maps of the world from 1945 to the present day, including UN maps of conflict areas and disputed territories.

Index

Page numbers written in **boldface** refer to pictures or captions.